AF270459

THE BEST OF WORLD SOCCER

THE BEST RIVALRIES OF WORLD SOCCER

BY CHRÖS MCDOUGALL

SportsZone

An Imprint of Abdo Publishing
abdobooks.com

abdobooks.com

Published by Abdo Publishing, a division of ABDO, PO Box 398166, Minneapolis, Minnesota 55439. Copyright © 2024 by Abdo Consulting Group, Inc. International copyrights reserved in all countries. No part of this book may be reproduced in any form without written permission from the publisher. SportsZone™ is a trademark and logo of Abdo Publishing.

Printed in the United States of America, North Mankato, Minnesota.
102023
012024

Editor: Luke Hanlon
Series Designers: Karli Kruse and Joshua Olson

Library of Congress Control Number: 2023939433

Publisher's Cataloging-in-Publication Data

Names: McDougall, Chrös, author.
Title: The best rivalries of world soccer / by Chrös McDougall
Description: Minneapolis, Minnesota: Abdo Publishing, 2024 | Series: The best of world soccer | Includes online resources and index.
Identifiers: ISBN 9781098292287 (lib. bdg.) | ISBN 9798384910220 (ebook)
Subjects: LCSH: Soccer--Juvenile literature. | Professional sports--Juvenile literature. | Soccer Teams--Juvenile literature. | Soccer matches--Juvenile literature. | Soccer--Records--Juvenile literature.
Classification: DDC 796.334--dc23

TABLE OF CONTENTS

CHAPTER 1

LOS CLÁSICOS

A pass from Lionel Messi, considered by many to be the world's best player, set up Barcelona teammate Andrés Iniesta for the opening goal just seven minutes into the game. Karim Benzema, one of the world's most dangerous strikers, answered with a goal for Real Madrid only 13 minutes later.

More than 85,000 fans erupted in cheers at Madrid's Santiago Bernabéu Stadium. Matches between Spain's most powerful men's club teams are nicknamed El Clásico, or "The Classic." And this meeting on March 23, 2014, soon became one of the most memorable El Clásicos in the rivalry's long and storied history.

The Frenchman Benzema, dressed in the iconic all-white uniform of Real Madrid, put his team up 2–1 with a right-footed goal in the 24th minute. Just before halftime, Messi, in the blue-and-dark-red-striped shirt of Barcelona, lurked in Madrid's penalty area. When the opportunity came, the Argentine slipped the ball into the net. At 26 years old, Messi now had 19 goals against Real Madrid. That made him the leading scorer in El Clásico history.

However, Real Madrid had its own superstar with a claim for being the world's best player in Cristiano Ronaldo. And in the 55th minute, the Portuguese forward scored on a penalty kick. That put Madrid up 3–2. However, Ronaldo's teammate, the skilled but at times reckless Spanish defender Sergio Ramos, was sent off with a red card a few minutes later. Messi tied the game 3–3 on the ensuing penalty. Then, in the 84th minute, he added another goal from the penalty spot to secure the hat trick and the 4–3 win. It was another iconic El Clásico.

EL CLÁSICO

Soccer rivalries develop for many reasons. Some begin because teams are neighbors in the same city. Others involve teams from cities that frequently compare themselves in areas such as business or culture. Sometimes fans from certain teams have opposing values. Often rivalries simply emerge because teams find themselves facing off in big games over and over again.

Lionel Messi kisses the Barcelona badge after scoring the game-winning goal against Real Madrid in 2014.

Cristiano Ronaldo scored 18 goals for Real Madrid in 30 career appearances against Barcelona. Only Messi has scored more El Clásico goals.

The Barcelona–Real Madrid rivalry has it all. The teams come from Spain's two biggest cities. The *real* in Real Madrid's name is Spanish for "royal." As a result, the team is often linked with Spanish nationalism. On the field, no team has been better. Real Madrid won the first five European Cups, beginning in 1955–56. In 2022 the team known as *Los Blancos* ("The Whites") won the tournament, now called the Champions League, for a record 14th time.

Barcelona, meanwhile, represents the Catalonia region of Spain. Many Catalans believe their region should be its own country. The soccer team serves as a symbol of that independent spirit. Barcelona has won five European titles, ranking fifth overall.

With their recognizable uniforms, famous stadiums, and long histories of fielding star players, Barcelona and Real Madrid are two of the most iconic sports teams in the world. The teams met on the field for the first time on May 13, 1902. Their rivalry grew during the 1950s when both teams tried to sign Alfredo Di Stéfano. The star striker agreed to join Barcelona only to instead sign with Madrid. He then became a key player in Madrid's early run of European titles.

In the decades that followed, both teams frequently featured some of the best players in the world. At no point was that truer than in the 2010s, when Barcelona had Messi and Madrid had Ronaldo. With the teams' history, success, cultures, and stars, it's no surprise that El Clásico often draws tens of millions of viewers around the world.

MORE AND MORE CLÁSICOS

Barcelona and Real Madrid's El Clásico is perhaps soccer's most famous rivalry. It's also just one of many rivalries to use *Clásico* in its nickname. Buenos Aires is Argentina's largest city.

Emotions often run hot when Barcelona and Real Madrid meet in El Clásico.

As soccer was spreading around the world in the early 1900s, workers there founded the men's clubs Boca Juniors and River Plate. Boca continued to be the city's working-class club. River Plate grew to represent more affluent residents. For many years, Boca was known for playing an aggressive, physical style. River Plate developed a skilled passing style. These differing styles only added to the tension when the neighbors developed into two of South America's most successful teams.

As Argentina grew into a global power in international men's soccer, many of the country's biggest stars spent time with one of the clubs. Diego Maradona, the star of the 1986 World Cup, was Boca's most famous player. Di Stéfano was among the stars who once played for River Plate. Games between the two clubs became known as *Superclásicos*. The atmosphere in the stadium when these teams play is often described as being as intense as any game in the world.

A few thousand miles north in Mexico, fans take sides on *El Super Clásico*. Club América is the biggest of the three

Passionate Boca Juniors fans climb a fence that surrounds parts of the field in their home stadium during a game against River Plate in 2018.

Fernando González of Club América, *left*, fouls Gael Sandoval of Chivas during a game in 2019.

teams in Mexico City, the country's capital. Club Deportivo Guadalajara, better known as Chivas, plays 340 miles (550 km) west in Guadalajara. Both began as amateur teams. Then they helped start Mexico's first professional league in 1943–44. Chivas became known for signing only players who had been born in Mexico. América embraced a flashier image built on foreign stars. As the teams developed into Mexico's two most successful and popular clubs, their different styles only increased the tension. For many fans, defeating their rival is just as important as winning the league.

There are other Clásicos in Latin America. Paraguay has its own *Superclásico* between Asunción teams Olimpio and Cerro Porteño. Many other rivalries incorporate the name, too. The *Clásico Universitario* in Chile features Universidad de Chile and Universidad Católica, both of Santiago. Colombia's *Clásico Capitalino* is contested between Cali and Medellín. Meanwhile, among national teams, Chile and Peru play in the *Clásico del Pacifico*. Argentina and Uruguay play the *Clásico Rioplatense*. And matches between Argentina and Brazil are nicknamed *Superclásico Sudamericano*.

CHAPTER 2

EUROPEAN RIVALRIES

The first official rules for soccer were written down in England in the mid-1800s. It didn't take long for the British to spread their game around the world. The sport took off in Milan, the biggest city in northern Italy, during the early 1900s.

In 1899 a pair of Englishmen created the Milan Football and Cricket Club. The men's team today is known as AC Milan. Despite the team's English founders, Milan grew to proudly embrace its Italian identity. However, some of the club's members wanted the team to accept more international players. So in 1908, they left to create a new team called Internazionale, or Inter Milan. Both teams have long since been open to foreign players. Still, that initial disagreement set the stage for Italy's most famous rivalry.

AC Milan historically represented the city's working class. Inter Milan fans tended to be wealthier. Both found much success on the field. AC Milan won its 19th Serie A title as the champion of Italy's top league in 2021–22. That matched Inter for the second most. Only Juventus, based in Turin, has won more. AC Milan has bettered Inter in European competition, however. While Inter won its third Champions League title in 2010, it still trailed Milan's seven. Real Madrid is the only team that has won the competition more.

One unique aspect of the AC Milan–Inter rivalry is that the teams have shared a home stadium, Stadio Giuseppe Meazza, commonly called the San Siro, since 1947. When the two powers play each other there, the game is nicknamed the *Derby della Madonnina.*

RIVALRIES ACROSS ENGLAND

As the home nation of soccer, England has some of the oldest men's club teams in the world. And with hundreds of teams in a country roughly the size of Alabama, rivals are always close by. In fact, many cities have more than one team. When neighbors meet, it's called a derby (pronounced *DAR-be*).

Manchester United players, *in red*, taunt Liverpool's Daniel Sturridge during a game in 2014

No two English teams have played in more big games than Liverpool and Manchester United, which are based just 35 miles (56 km) apart in northwest England. Liverpool dominated the sport in the 1970s and 1980s. Under manager Sir Alex Ferguson, United emerged in the 1990s as England's top team. The teams' history and popularity have made their games among the most anticipated in England. The cities' closeness only adds to the tension, as fans from both sides view theirs as the best city in the region.

Games between England's biggest clubs draw attention from around the world. To many English fans, however, the most important rivalry might instead be the local derby. Liverpool has been playing city rival Everton in the Merseyside derby since 1894. The match gets its name from River Mersey, which runs through the city. The Manchester derby between United and Manchester City is ever older. However, it wasn't until the 2010s that it truly became competitive. Wealthy new owners helped City go from an also-ran to a European power. Perhaps no game signaled City's arrival more than one in which it thrashed United 6–1 in 2011.

Fierce rivalries can be found in every corner of England. Newcastle and Sunderland face off in the Tyne–Wear derby in the northeast. Portsmouth and Southampton contest the South Coast derby. Birmingham in central England has the

Physical altercations between Tottenham Hotspur, *white*, and Arsenal, *red*, are not uncommon in North London derbies.

Second City derby between Aston Villa and Birmingham City. Meanwhile, the Greater London area boasts more than a dozen professional teams. Chelsea emerged as London's most successful team in the 2000s, making the Blues a natural rival for many teams. However, many say the North London derby between Arsenal and Tottenham Hotspur is the city's fiercest matchup, as the teams' stadiums are just four miles (6 km) apart.

THE OLD FIRM

North of England, Celtic and Rangers, both of Glasgow, Scotland, have what might be the world's most heated rivalry. The teams met on the field for the first time in 1888. The fans' ill will for one another goes much deeper than a simple crosstown feud, however.

Fans of each team traditionally differ in their religious, political, and national identities. Celtic is seen as the city's Catholic team, and many fans identify more with Ireland than with the United Kingdom. Meanwhile, Rangers fans tend to

be Protestants and proudly British. These differences have led to conflicts in daily life. And when the teams meet in the Old Firm derby, many fans view the game as an extension of these disputes.

All the while, the rivalry's intensity is supercharged by the fact that Celtic and Rangers have been by far the two best teams in Scotland. Both clubs have won the Scottish league over 50 times. No other team has more than four. Former Celtic striker Henrik Larsson once said of the Old Firm, "That was the best atmosphere and those were the most fierce encounters I ever played in." However, that intensity has sometimes led to violence and even deaths among fans.

BATTLE FOR WOMEN'S SUPREMACY

For many years, women didn't have many opportunities to play soccer. The women's game began developing at the international level during the 1980s, and the first Women's World Cup was held in 1991. Professional chances slowly followed. The first edition of what is now the European Women's Champions League was held in 2001–02. However, most of the participants would be unfamiliar to those who followed men's soccer. That soon began to change.

Olympique Lyonnais, better known as Lyon, emerged as a top men's team in France during the 2000s. The club's women's team, meanwhile, became a European power. Lyon won its first Women's Champions League in 2011. Within a decade, it had added six more. Being backed by ar

Defender Wendie Renard took over as Lyon's captain in 2013.

established men's club had advantages. Lyon was able to provide its women's team with better resources and funding than most independent women's teams had. As a result, top players, such as Norwegian forward Ada Hegerberg and French defender Wendie Renard, were drawn to the club. And the more Lyon won, the better it seemed to get.

It wasn't long before other men's clubs took notice of Lyon's success. They realized that with some investment, they too could have successful women's teams. Now some of the biggest men's teams in Europe are going all in on women's soccer.

No women's team has grown more rapidly than Barcelona. Though it had been around since 1988, the Barcelona women's team became professional only in 2015. With the support of the

Lyon's Ada Hegerberg celebrates after scoring a goal against Barcelona in the 2022 Women's Champions League final.

Barcelona captain Vicky Losada lifts the Women's Champions League trophy in 2021.

storied men's club, Barcelona soon became Spain's dominant women's team.

In 2019 Barcelona reached its first Women's Champions League final. It faced Lyon. A Hegerberg hat trick within the first 30 minutes led Lyon to a 4–1 win. But two years later, Barcelona was back. This time, the Spanish team dominated Chelsea of England to win its first European title.

To many, that final was telling. Both teams were associated with powerful men's clubs. Many experts predicted that all the top women's teams would soon be like this. And no team's future looked brighter than Barcelona's. The Lyon players heard this talk. "There was women's football before Barcelona, and it was played here for years," Hegerberg said.

The two women's powers met in the 2022 Women's Champions League final. It was one of the most anticipated games in the tournament's history. And Lyon showed its dynasty wasn't over yet. Hegerberg helped the French team score three early goals on the way to a 3–1 win.

CHAPTER 3

AROUND THE WORLD

Tens of thousands of fans march into the stadium. They chant and sing. As kickoff nears, they raise what's called a tifo. It's a giant 20,000-square-foot (1,858-sq-m) banner showing scenes of the city's soccer tradition. This isn't a game between historic clubs in Europe or South America, though.

It takes place in the Pacific Northwest of the United States and Canada.

The Seattle Sounders joined MLS in 2009. Two years later, the Portland Timbers followed. The Vancouver Whitecaps also arrived in 2011. Each year, the teams battle for the Cascadia Cup. It's named for a mountain range in the region. And this three-way contest has quickly become one of the fiercest rivalries in North American soccer.

PORTLAND THORNS VS. OL REIGN

The Portland Thorns and OL Reign of Seattle first met in 2013. That was also the first year of the National Women's Soccer League (NWSL). Portland won in front of a rowdy home crowd of 16,479 that day. Their games continue to be among the league's most anticipated each year.

Three Portland Timbers players hold up logs after each scored in a 3–2 win against the Sounders in 2013.

The Cascadia Cup has all the makings of a good rivalry. Portland, Seattle, and Vancouver are the three biggest cities in the region. People have long argued over which city is the best, sports or otherwise. The soccer rivalry also has a surprising history. Teams from the three cities have been playing each other since the 1970s. In fact, fans created the Cascadia Cup in 2004, when all three cities had popular teams in the same minor league.

Each team has passionate fans and a unique culture. Games between the Sounders and Timbers are the most intense. Seattle is the flashiest of the Cascadia teams. The Sounders often wear brightly colored jerseys. Their games feature some of MLS's biggest crowds. Portland fans pride themselves on having a more unconventional style. They play in a converted baseball stadium. After each goal, a lumberjack named Timber Joey cuts a piece off a giant log. After the match he gives it to the player who scored.

PAULISTA DERBY

Sprawled over 576 square miles (1,493 sq km), the city of São Paulo, Brazil, is home to more than 10 million people. The metropolitan area has a population of 19 million. That makes it the biggest city in the Southern Hemisphere. It also features one of South America's most famous soccer rivalries.

In a country famous for its soccer, São Paulo is home to four of Brazil's biggest teams. Corinthians, Palmeiras, Santos, and São Paulo are all regular contenders in the country's top league, called Serie A. Anytime two of them meet, it's a big deal.

No games are bigger than those between Corinthians and Palmeiras. Founded in 1910, Corinthians is one of Brazil's most successful teams. Palmeiras began four years later. Soccer was still new to Brazil at the time. Corinthians has its roots in São Paulo's Spanish community, while Palmeiras has Italian roots. Over the years the teams grew to represent more than these ethnic groups—while meeting in many memorable matches.

Derbies are deeply ingrained in South American soccer. As nations grew there, many tended to have one dominant city. Boca Juniors and River Plate became the powers in Buenos Aires, Argentina. In Uruguay, Nacional and Peñarol are the biggest teams in Montevideo. Meanwhile, farther north, soccer began to gain popularity

Felipe Melo of Palmeiras showcases the intense emotion that often comes out among players and fans when his team plays Corinthians.

in Colombia during the 1940s. The country has two huge rivalries. Bogotá has Santa Fe and Millonarios. Medellín has a club named after the city. Its biggest rival is fellow Medellín club Atlético Nacional.

KINGS OF EGYPT

History was made in Egypt's Cairo International Stadium on November 27, 2020. Al Ahly and Zamalek, the two biggest clubs in Egypt's largest city, met in the African Champions League final. It marked the first time the final featured two teams from

Amro El Soulia (17) of Al Ahly celebrates after scoring against Zamalek in the 2020 African Champions League final.

the same country. And they just happened to be two of the fiercest rivals in global soccer.

Al Ahly is Egypt's most successful team. It was founded by students and workers in 1907. The country's other top club, Zamalek, has long been associated with nobility. One of the two teams almost always wins the league. Now they were meeting for the biggest prize in Africa.

The COVID-19 pandemic prevented the teams' passionate fans from attending the game. They missed an intense meeting. Al Ahly scored early, only for Zamalek to tie the game 30 minutes later. The game stayed that way until the 88th minute. That's when Al Ahly's Mohamed Magdy placed a volley into the corner of the net. Already Africa's most successful team, Al Ahly won another Champions League title in the sweetest way possible.

CITY OR VICTORY?

Not all rivalries are built on history. Women's club soccer is still relatively new. In 2008 Melbourne Victory was founded in Australia's second-largest city. Melbourne City followed a few years later in 2015. The teams were instant, natural rivals in Australia's top league.

An undefeated first season for City no doubt stung for Victory fans. Both teams are regularly among the best in the

Katie Bowen of Melbourne City, *right*, puts in a physical tackle on Melbourne Victory's Lia Privitelli during a meeting between the teams in 2023.

league. One of their most memorable games came in the 2023 playoff semifinals. City came back from 3–1 down to tie the game in the 97th minute, only to lose in a dramatic shootout.

CHAPTER 4

NATIONAL PRIDE

The men's national teams from England and Scotland met on a soccer field for the first time in 1872. The match ended in a 0–0 tie. While that game wasn't very memorable, it did mark the beginning of the oldest international soccer rivalry.

England is considered the birthplace of soccer. Along with Northern Ireland, Scotland, and Wales, it is part of the United Kingdom. But because of the sport's long history there, the four nations are allowed to compete separately in international soccer.

England is by far the UK's largest nation. It has also been the most successful in soccer. Scotland has at times challenged its neighbor. In 1966 England won its lone World Cup. But just one year later, Scotland came down to London and stunned England 3–2 at Wembley Stadium. The teams have met twice in the European Championship. England won the first meeting 2–0 in 1996. When the teams played in 2021, they drew 0–0. In recent years, the rivalry has renewed on the women's side.

RIVALRY RENEWED

Competing on home soil, England beat West Germany in the 1966 men's World Cup final. It was one of many memorable games between the two teams. A new era began in 2022. In front of a record home crowd of 87,192, England's women beat Germany to win the European title. It was the first major championship for England's women.

The teams met to open the group stage at the 2019 Women's World Cup, and England won 2–1.

SOUTH AMERICAN SUPREMACY

Brazil had emerged as a passionate soccer country by the time it hosted the 1950 men's World Cup. Instead of celebrating victory on home soil, however, the Brazilians were

Pelé holds up the World Cup trophy in 1970 after Brazil won the tournament for the third time.

left heartbroken by a South American neighbor. It wasn't
Argentina. Instead, Uruguay beat Brazil to win its second World
Cup title.

Though Uruguay proved to be South America's first world
champion, the rivalry between Argentina and Brazil would
soon define soccer on the continent. The teams first played in
1914. Over the years, each side has enjoyed periods of success.
Argentina held an edge in the early years. Then Brazil won
three World Cups from 1958 to 1970. Playing with an attacking
flair and featuring the iconic goal scorer Pelé, the Brazilians
became popular around the world.

This didn't sit well with the Argentines. The team, known
more for its grittier playing style, was still seeking its first world
title. In 1974, Brazil and Argentina met for the first time at a
World Cup, with Brazil winning their second-round game 2–1.
The teams met again four years later, when Argentina hosted
the tournament. This time they played to a goalless draw
in a second-round game marred by violence. It was an ugly
result, but for Argentina all that mattered was staying in the
tournament. Soon after, the Argentines broke through to win
their first World Cup. And eight years later, in 1986, Argentina
won again. The dominant performance from forward Diego
Maradona there sparked another rivalry. People today still
debate whether Pelé or Maradona was the best player ever.

After 1986 there was no question that Argentina and Brazil were global soccer powers. Brazil added additional World Cup titles in 1994 and 2002. No country has more than Brazil's five championships. However, Argentina is not far behind after winning its third title in 2022. Brazil and Argentina have met only four times in World Cup play, with the last being in 1990. Instead, their most anticipated meetings typically come during World Cup qualifying and in Copa América, the South American championship.

In 2021 Brazil was the Copa América host and defending champion. Argentina, seeking its first tournament championship in 28 years, sneaked past Brazil 1–0 in the final. That gave Argentina 15 Copa América titles, tied with Uruguay for the most. For Argentina fans, the win was especially sweet, as it was the first major title for superstar Lionel Messi. One year later, he led the team to another World Cup title. And now when fans

Winning the Copa América is always an achievement, but beating Brazil in the final added significance to Argentina's win in 2021.

debate whether Pelé or Maradona was the best, many include Messi in the conversation, too.

USMNT VS. MEXICO

The US and Mexico men's soccer teams played for the first time in 1934. By the 1950s, however, the countries' soccer journeys had split. Mexico had built a strong tradition. Meanwhile, soccer's popularity remained behind many other sports in the United States.

In 1990 the United States qualified for its first World Cup in 40 years. Soon the rivalry with Mexico was back on, and it was bigger than ever. On the field, Mexico was usually the better team. And the games between the teams often turned nasty.

The play often becomes chippy and physical when Mexico and the United States meet on a soccer field.

However, at the 2002 World Cup, a savvy US team beat Mexico 2–0 in the round of 16 in South Korea. The win marked a turning point in the rivalry. That match was also one of many 2–0 wins for the Americans around this time. US fans cheerfully nicknamed these wins *"Dos a Cero"*—Spanish for "two to zero."

In World Cup qualifying, Mexico hosts its games at Estadio Azteca. The stadium is in Mexico City, which is at a higher altitude than many players are used to. It's also massive. Upward of 100,000 fans, known for their noise and intensity, create a hostile environment for visitors. Through 2022, the United States still had never won a competitive game there. In 2001 the United States created its own home-field advantage in World Cup qualifiers against Mexico. Starting that year, the games were held in Columbus, Ohio. The smaller stadium, seating fewer than 20,000 fans, was packed with passionate US fans, creating an electric atmosphere. It didn't hurt that the weather in Columbus was often cold. However, for US fans the most memorable part of the 2001, 2005, 2009, and 2013 games in Columbus was the score line: all 2–0 US wins.

USWNT VS. EVERYBODY

In 1991 the United States beat Norway 2–1 in the final of the first Women's World Cup. That was only the beginning of the first great rivalry in women's soccer.

Norway got the best of the Americans in some key matches. The Norwegians beat the United States in the 1995 World Cup semifinal, then won the championship. Norway also beat the US team in the 2000 Olympic gold-medal game.

Still, the United States remained a power. And as Norway faded away, other challengers emerged. The 1996 Olympics were the first to include women's soccer. Many saw China as the sport's next great team. However, superstar Sun Wen and China couldn't get past the United States in the gold-medal game. Then, in one of the sport's iconic matches, the US team outlasted China in a shootout in the 1999 Women's World Cup final.

Superstar Marta and Brazil stepped up next. The Americans topped Brazil in the 2004 Olympic gold-medal game. However, Brazil responded by thumping the US team 4–0 in the 2007 World Cup semifinals. Marta scored twice in that winning effort, which marked a low point for the US team.

The United States got revenge in the quarterfinals of the 2011 World Cup. However, a new rivalry began when Japan stunned the Americans in the final. But once again, the United States came back. It beat Japan in the finals of the 2012 Olympics and 2015 World Cup. Before long the US team had four World Cup wins and four Olympic gold medals. No country had enjoyed more success.

Abby Wambach (20) celebrates after the United States defeated Japan in the 2015 World Cup final.

One rival never went away, though. The United States and Sweden often seemed to meet in major tournaments. Eventually, Sweden handed the US team some of its worst losses. That included penalty-shootout defeats in the 2016 Olympic quarterfinals and the 2023 World Cup round of 16. Both marked the United States' earliest defeat in each tournament. Still, in 43 all-time meetings, Sweden had only 13 wins.

The emotion often goes deeper than the final score when Japan and South Korea meet for a soccer game.

ASIAN POWERS

Only a narrow strait separates the Korean peninsula and Japan. In 1910 Japan took control of its neighbor. For the next three and a half decades, the Japanese tried to wipe out Korean culture, often in brutal ways. Finally, at the end of World War II in 1945, Korea was freed, creating the countries of North Korea and South Korea.

That history was still fresh in 1954, when the men's soccer teams from Japan and South Korea met for the first time. The winner of a two-game series would qualify for that year's World Cup. Both games were held in Japan. Before the trip, the South Korean president told the players that if they lost, they shouldn't come back. Thankfully for the players, they won the series.

South Korea had become a regular at the World Cup by the time Japan qualified for the first time in 1998. Having long been rivals, the neighbors became Asia's strongest teams, too. Then, in 2002, they joined together to host the World Cup. It was the first time two countries had shared hosting duties. At that tournament, South Korea became the first Asian nation to reach the semifinals.

Soccer has captivated fans around the world for more than a century. Rivalries are a huge reason why. No matter where they're being played, rivalry games provide great drama.

GLOSSARY

AFFLUENT
Having a lot of money or wealth.

ALTITUDE
The distance above sea level.

AMATEUR
Something that is done for fun rather than as a job.

CLUB
The team a player competes with outside of his or her national team.

DYNASTY
A team that has an extended period of success, usually winning multiple championships in the process.

HAT TRICK
Three or more goals by the same player in one game.

NATIONALISM
A strong identification with one's own nation, often at the expense of others.

NOBILITY
People in a social class that typically ranks just below royalty.

PANDEMIC
A widespread outbreak of a disease that affects a large portion of the population.

PENALTY AREA
The box in front of the goal where a player is granted a penalty kick if he or she is fouled.

PENALTY KICK
A play in which a shooter faces a goalkeeper alone; it is used to decide tied tournament games or as a result of a foul.

PROFESSIONAL
Something that is done as a job.

SHOOTOUT
A series of penalty kicks held after extra time to decide who wins a game.

MORE INFORMATION

BOOKS

Avise, Jonathan. *Great Soccer Debates*. Minneapolis, MN: Abdo Publishing, 2019.

Hewson, Anthony K. *GOATs of Soccer*. Minneapolis, MN: Abdo Publishing, 2022.

Marthaler, Jon. *The Best Teams of World Soccer*. Minneapolis, MN: Abdo Publishing, 2024.

ONLINE RESOURCES

To learn more about soccer rivalries, please visit **abdobooklinks.com** or scan this QR code. These links are routinely monitored and updated to provide the most current information available.

INDEX

ABOUT THE AUTHOR

Chrös McDougall is an author, editor, and sportswriter who regularly covers soccer as well as Olympic and Paralympic sports. Among his assignments over the years have been reporting on the first game at the new Wembley Stadium in London for the Associated Press and covering the US women's soccer team at the 2021 Olympics in Tokyo, Japan, for TeamUSA.org. He lives in Minneapolis with his wife, his soccer-loving son and daughter, and a well-meaning boxer named Eira.